Lick Like a Lesbian

Lick Like a Lesbian

Wise Cracks

Library of Congress Control Number: 2020910760
ISBN: Hardcover   978-1-9845-9453-2
                 Softcover   978-1-9845-9452-5
                 eBook   978-1-9845-9451-8

Print information available on the last page.

Rev. date: 06/17/2020

To order additional copies of this book, contact:
Xlibris
UK TFN: 0800 0148620 (Toll Free inside the UK)
UK Local: 02036 956328 (+44 20 3695 6328 from outside the UK)
www.Xlibrispublishing.co.uk
Orders@Xlibrispublishing.co.uk
811281

Lick Like a Lesbian

An informed but fun guide on how

to perform great oral sex

Easy-to-follow steps gently brought to

you by the Wise Cracks Team

The Wise Cracks Team is made up of:

Author and potential comedian: GDC from the UK

Illustrious illustrator: Caty Blaak from the Netherlands

Supporting us in this slightly creative spin on how to perfect oral sex was a great and we must say eager group of volunteers from around the world who put in considerable time to test the techniques contained in *Lick Like a Lesbian*. What a team, we would like to thank all of them.

And we all need a team, right? As we all know it is highly unlikely that even Fanny Cradock tasted all of her own cakes!

WISE CRACKS Ltd.

So if you are ready then follow us.

CONTENTS

CONTENTS

CHAPTER 1

The Opening

Fly like a bird, swim like a fish, fuck like a rabbit, and run like a horse. Not many of us are in the same league when it comes to keeping up with these natural specialists, try as we might. But what about "lick like a lesbian"? Again, it's a tall order—a stretch of the imagination, maybe—but if we are honest, who doesn't want to be able to do that? They say nobody does it better, possibly. Well this pocket-sized, tongue-in-cheek user guide on how to perfectly perform ten much-loved oral sex acts has been passionately put together by the Wise Cracks Team with you and your partner in mind. So, while we may not be able to show you how to fly like a bird or swim like a fish and so on, we can indeed teach you how to lick like a lesbian.

This amusing yet eloquent guide provides an exciting cocktail of fun and enhanced techniques that will take you on an exploratory journey both around and inside your partner's genitals to produce a culinary three-Michelin-star equivalent to oral sexual delight. All you have to do is choose your favourites from our menu or indulge yourself a little in all of this fine sexual dining experience, which is here for everyone.

The techniques are based on tried-and-tested results delivered to you by a group of very happy volunteers who gave up endless evenings of television, going down the pub, and posh eating out so they could take part in a purely voluntary process which was able to produce extraordinary results. The Wise Cracks Team would like to recognise and pay thanks to the pure dedication and thoroughness the volunteers provided.

As you are now nicely chilled and reading this and possibly a bit horny, we assume that you are also a bit curious as to how you can achieve that perfect oral experience. If the answer is yes, and we are sure it is, then all you need to do now is follow the simple steps, diagrams, and tips herein that will guide you both and provide all you need to know for delivering and sharing the perfect oral orgasm.

Even if you don't have a tongue like a giraffe or a pussy like a New York pastrami sandwich, there is no need to worry; we will show you how to get the best out of this stirring and stimulating form of lovemaking.

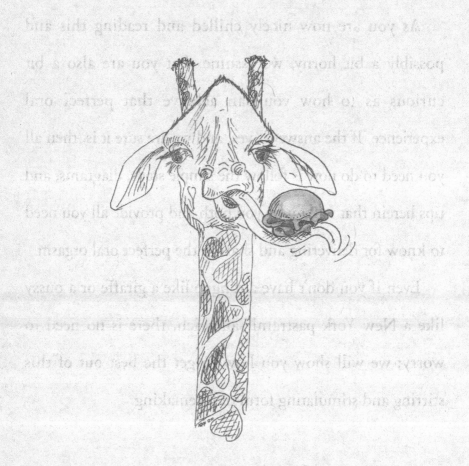

**And remember, "If you can't lick the one you
love, then love the one you lick." Enjoy!**

CHAPTER 2

Observations

Many would agree that oral sex is probably the most intimate form of lovemaking you can share with your partner. Mastering the art of oral sex can elevate your lovemaking and do wonders for the intimacy levels and closeness in your relationship. It will bond you forever. The expression "it's the best thing since sliced bread" is liberally showered upon things we enjoy doing and recommend to others, but have you ever wondered what actually *is* the very best thing since sliced bread? Well wonder no more because this is it. Administered properly, it is unbeatable. Believe us, oral sex is *it*. And once you have perfected it, OMG, sex does not get any better. We are sure those who have had the pleasure of such carnal ecstasy will totally agree. Simply put, it is a myriad of techniques and indulgences blended by passion and a willingness to pleasure which delivers the finest love cocktail ever. It's an art—an art that is there for all of us to soak up and enjoy.

The aim of this guide is to steer you through the preparation needed for many sensational oral sexual experiences. In addition, it will also describe to you how to hit the highs and then the even higher highs using the many oral techniques that you can perform with your partner. It will also be fun, of course, as everything in life should be.

Further, for the guys, since we are not talking about traditional intercourse, you don't need a big cock, which is good news for the slightly less fortunate amongst you. What you do need, though, is a willing partner, patience, a desire to please, and the basic techniques, which are provided to you in this guide.

It's worth pointing out that there are no exams or tests at the end of this read. Your only judges are your partner and yourself. So don't worry: you can continue to refer to or practice these described techniques as often or as little as you need to. Take from this book what you will and use what works for you. We are all different, so keep going until you find what techniques suit you both best. It's what you enjoy that matters.

One thing to bear in mind, though, is that staring close up at somebody else's genitalia is going to produce a wide range of emotions depending on the person or persons doing the staring. Whether you find it scary, funny, or beautiful, or it simply makes you hornier more moist this guide doesn't really prepare you for that part. You have to work this one out for yourself. The Wise Cracks Team can only suggest that you learn to enjoy every aspect of the experience. You could always start to become more familiar with your partner's genital details before oral sex by taking photos and discussing them with each other, or by getting naked and having live viewing and chat sessions beforehand. It's your choice as to how you try to overcome any shyness and understand what you are looking at. Any practice and familiarisation can only be a good thing.

However, anybody with a wildish bush may want to reach for the scissors and then the razor to tidy up a bit before any intimate chat to try to minimise any chance of a negative outcome. Just kidding! As we said earlier, we are all different, and that is what makes oral sex fun and unique.

CHAPTER 3

House Rules

Good housekeeping is important, so this guide has been sensitively and carefully prepared by the Wise Cracks Team to cover the following areas:

- Hygiene and safety. It's not much, and it's not meant to make life tougher than it is. This section covers just the essentials. You will thank us for it in the end.

- Selecting a partner. Who or what make the best lickers?

- What to do with your pets. These are just recommendations; you should consider the welfare of your pets and follow any applicable animal welfare laws at all times.

- Getting warmed up. This is important, as it's not always easy to get going for some. We describe some simple steps here that will ensure a positive outcome and get you both in the mood.

CHAPTER 4

Hygiene and Safety

Sexual disease can be spread from having unprotected oral sex if care is not taken. So before we get into the more exciting sections of this guide, we need to address the importance of hygiene and safety, as these are critical to your well-being and enjoyment. Observing hygiene and safety recommendations is also the right thing to do; it shows you have respect for your partner and that you take care of and respect each other. This in itself provides assurance and will help relax both of you. A major part of successful oral sex is being able to relax and be comfortable with what's taking place between you. Hygiene plays a big part in that success.

Guys

So, guys, let's deal with the importance of your hygiene and safety first.

First, your face. Let's make sure your face is clean. Immediately beforehand, you need to wash your face in clean, warm water. Creams and aftershaves can irritate sensitive genital areas. I know for you these types of facial products are all about heightening the senses, and there is nothing wrong with where you are coming from, but on this occasion, you need to wear them somewhere else rather than on your face. Trust us.

Your partner's genitals are guaranteed to be very sensitive, and the aftershave or cream you may be wearing on your face could cause irritation. There is a chance that, after you have been rubbing it around her naughty bits for half an hour or so, it could cause some inflammation of the lips—both yours and hers. Nobody wants that, as it removes some fun from the whole process, and she may not let you in for a repeat performance. So, guys, no aftershave on the face, okay? Simply rinse your face in warm water beforehand. We recommend you do not use soap. Take your time to moisturise your skin with the natural minerals in the water. This is the bit where you need to chill. Take your time and look in the mirror if you have to—but only occasionally. Remember, you have a job to do, so no self-gratification yet.

If you are sporting a beard or moustache, we suggest this is trimmed and tidy but more importantly it is washed clean and free from debris.

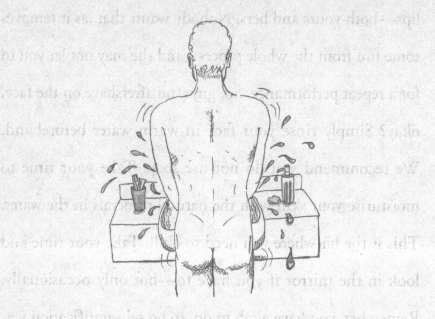

Now on to dick cleanliness. A very important aspect of success with oral sex is to have a spotlessly clean and sweet-smelling dick, so zero odours, okay? There is no hiding it. Failure in this department will see you banished to the man cave or garage, and you will never, ever get back in there. So pay attention.

Again, we use only warm water. Not too hot or you could blister a bit which doesn't look so good, plus you don't want to run the risk of minor burns which could trigger an annoying trip to A&E for some treatment. So, okay, you have run the water. Now use a tiny bit of soap and rub the soap around the end of your dick and along the shaft. Pull back the foreskin and gently soap it up making sure you get all the way around the rim, or helmet, or whatever you call it. Please don't start rubbing it too hard at this point, okay? Just take it nice and easy. You don't want to get to the main course ahead of time. Give it a good inspection as you go through the process by pulling it about a little and waving it back and forth. We cannot emphasise enough that it has to be 100 per cent squeaky clean.

Now, once you are satisfied it's clean, lower it into the bowl of warm water and gently rinse off all of the soap. As with the aftershave on your face in the previous section, it is vitally important that you are also soap free for the same good reasons. Also, you want to make sure that, during the act of having your dick sucked, the bubbles from the side of your partner's mouth are being generated by something other than residual soap that you left tucked away under your foreskin. Also, while you are about it, drop your balls in to the warm water for a bit of a rinse just to remove any saltiness from perspiration.

Once you are finished and you are sure you are soap free, simply dry off with a soft towel. It's important to pat dry and not rub. Please, again, avoid the temptation for any rubbing. Think of the potential for a bit of an unnecessary rash from chaffing—get the picture? After going to all of the trouble of scrubbing up meticulously, you don't want to cause any unwanted stress from a developing rash on your dick. Because if that's happening, she or he will spot it soon enough, and that could spell disaster. So always take your time and pamper your dick; it's worth it in the long run. Oh, one last thing—have a look in the mirror at your pubic hair. We are not saying you have to shave it all off like some gods do, as is the fashion nowadays, but at least make it neat and tidy so it's presentable.

Out-of-control Yiddish curls spiralling off in all directions is not nice. So tidy up a bit, okay? Be critical of your appearance. If you do need to reach for the scissors, then I am afraid you need to repeat the steps above on cleanliness and washing just in case a bit of pubic hair has become trapped somewhere nasty. Nobody wants to be surprised by that halfway through giving you a blowjob. You will know when it happens as well because the facial expression from the person giving the blowjob will change dramatically from eyebrows up (meaning "Oh, I am quite liking this! He was so clean. Ten out of ten for male grooming. Never seen his dick look so good"—that kind of thing) to eyebrows down and a squinted look on the face (meaning "What the fuck is that sharp wiry thing in my throat? God, I am going to gag!"). This is usually followed by your partner rushing off to the bathroom to rinse before making a quick call for a cab. All you end up with is a curt good night and, "Thank you for nearly choking me to death on your old bits of curly piano wire!" We don't think this is what you want, so try to take a bit of care.

Ladies

Now, ladies, it's your turn. Again, let's tackle your face first. We can deal with your pussy afterwards. Let's face it, you shouldn't have the same issues as the guys with beards and things, so I think we can keep it simple here.

Like the guys, though, once you remove any heavy make-up, do wash your face in warm water. It may be that, during oral sex, once you have the bit between your teeth so to speak, some skin products could rub off on him and cause irritation. It's highly unlikely that it's going to do any sustainable damage, but just to be sure keep make-up to an absolute minimum please. Another good tip is to remove any false eye lashes. During the heat of the moment when you are being pleasured, you could loose and possibly swallow one if it falls off and lands on his dick without anyone noticing. It may lead to gagging for all the wrong reasons, so it's probably best to play safe and remove them beforehand.

Pussy cleanliness: well you can imagine how serious this is. We don't want any traces of acidy flavours lurking in the folds of skin or flaps generally, nothing that would provide a curt sharpness on the tongue causing it to retreat in a hurry back to where it came from. Neither do we want anything that might cause a tingling sensation on the tongue similar to the experience you get when you put your tongue on one of those electric fly swatting bats. No, it has to be clean and shiny like just-washed fruit. It's got to look beautiful, smell beautiful, and taste totally yummy. So, drop those knickers and prepare to bathe, rinse, or shower it properly. Do whatever is needed. Please—no short cuts by giving it a quick swipe with a baby wipe or a wet wipe either; it's just not the same. Firstly, they are perfumed, and secondly, they have a rather unpleasant taste. Try it if you don't believe us. If you want good results, then make the effort, okay?

Once the water temperature is right, then soak it, spray it, splash it, or do whatever it takes to get it looking, tasting, and smelling its best. Any half measures will only have negative impacts.

Again, as for pubic hair, we all have our preferences, and we are not going to advise you to trim it back or develop a landing strip or plat it or have some kind of Brazilian, okay? It's up to you what you do, but we suggest that, before things get started, you try to spot anything that might be a distraction during the act for your partner and deal with it. "Such as?" we hear you shout. Well, such as a wild offshoot of pubic hair that has developed the same attitude as that irritating shopping trolley—yes, the one that wanders off on its own like an out-of-control vine no matter how hard you try to get it under control. Our advice would be to cut out anything like this and to keep it out. This will be of real benefit if you venture down the route of having spurious, unplanned oral sex when speed is of the essence; for example, whilst in the car journeying home from the shops or the cinema or possibly on public transport like a train or a bus. Always try to be your best, as you never know when you might get lucky.

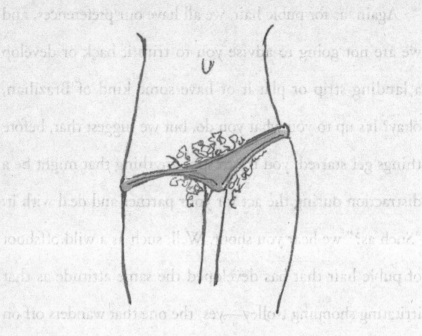

Teeth

For both men and women, it is also important to brush your teeth and rinse with mouthwash before and after the event. "Why before?" I hear you ask. Because it's not nice to be greeted by a beautifully formed mouth that still has signs of your last meal tucked in between the teeth. Come on, people, it's all about relaxation and comfort and image and cleanliness, and demonstration of that is important. So, pay attention, and let's make sure your teeth and your breath are clean enough to ensure your hygienist could take the day off work. This little twenty-second act goes a long way to making it obvious that you care.

CHAPTER 5

Selecting a Partner

What or who makes the best partner when it comes to oral sex? The answer is easy: it's most probably the one you love.

Sex in general is something you can learn to do well depending on how important it is to your relationship and how adventurous you both want to be. Being comfortable with the person you are with, though, is key. Oral sex is, in the opinion of the Wise Cracks Team, the most intimate and hence the most satisfying form of pleasure. Involve some chocolate and it becomes sumptuously electrifying. You may

25

not have much experience with oral sex up until now, and if you have, perhaps you have not achieved the level we reveal in this book, but the Wise Cracks Team are here to change all of that. We guarantee you will both learn and have fun trying. However, as for finding the G spot ... well, that's a different level all together.

CHAPTER 6

What to Do with Your Pets

We all love our pets, right? They love us. That said, we all know they can be curious beings. I am sure there have been instances when you and your partner are in the bedroom or garage, even maybe the man cave, and you are both as horny as hell and a seriously good shag is in full swing when all of a sudden you get a cold nose up your arse. It's a game changer, isn't it? It very abruptly stops you in your tracks. A scream goes out followed by a number of expletives like "Who left the fucking door open?" or "What the fuck?"

followed by a swift kick out to shift the beast from clinging to your leg. At first, it's unsuccessful. The dog doesn't budge. Momentarily you realise you are no longer in control here. He still stubbornly hangs on in there and basically ruins the whole experience. The annoying thing for you is that offers like this don't come along every day from your partner, and the dog has ruined it, and in the end, sadly, you simply have to stop.

So, if you have pets and love your pets, you need to get a grip of how much wandering licence you give them. Yes, you love them but not that much, okay? As part of warming up for one of our oral techniques, you have to lock them out! Whoever is the last person in the playroom should shut the door to keep the creature out. If the beast is in the room already, then take him or her out before the fun begins. If you have started already, please stop and remove the dog as soon as you see it. If you don't, then I guarantee it will get your gaze at every opportunity, which can be very off-putting, especially if you are on the vinegar strokes.

On the other hand, there may well be some of you out there who do a bit of bestiality. If you are into smearing chocolate sauce or peanut butter all over your private parts and surrendering to the slavering panting sloppy whatever, then the best of luck. That sort of thing is strictly not for us. Plus, it's probably illegal and definitely immoral and downright filthy. Take the bloody thing for a walk instead.

CHAPTER 7

Getting Warmed Up

For the best results, it may be better if you are already in a relationship since you are probably more familiar with each other's bodies in terms of sensitive and soft spots. However, if you are not, then oral sex can still be enjoyable, but you may need to take things a bit more slowly. That said, there are ways and means available on the internet that may be able to facilitate things for you, not that the Wise Cracks Team would know anything about that.

For the basis of this exercise, let's assume you and your partner are relatively new to the pleasures of oral sex but are still a bit shy and don't really talk much—or at all—about trying new things. This is okay, and it is the way it is for lots of people, which is why the Wise Cracks Team are here to help. So, the questions are: How do you approach the subject? How do you get the door—or legs, for that matter—open? Well, the good news is that you have options. Here are just a few to help you on your way.

- Surprise your partner by extending foreplay. How about getting started by kissing the feet and then work your way up the inside of the legs slowly caressing with your tongue until you have reached the genitals. At this point, unless your partner has objections, you just keep going, gently of course.

- You can also use some form of powered stimulation in the genital region to warm up your partner and then surprise him or her by quickly replacing it with your tongue, or combining the two when something else is expected.

- You could simply discuss oral sex over dinner with your partner. Suggest the possibility, the ramifications, and the desire. If he or she is comfortable with this very intimate sex act, then game on! If your partner is particularly horny, he or she may be receptive.

- You can, of course, provide your partner with a copy of this guide, which we are certain will have a positive impact.

- Or take the direct approach by pinning your partner down and giving him or her a good licking without taking no for an answer. This may not work for everybody, though. Remember to be gentle and respectful at all times. Please, however, don't do this if your relationship isn't secure enough to survive.

CHAPTER 8

The Ten Oral Techniques.

So, finally, with all of the do's and don'ts out of the way, we can move on to the main event: the ten oral techniques. These are the recommended approaches to providing great and potentially unrivalled pleasure when carrying out oral sex. It is our intention to guide you through the steps to ecstasy so that both you and your partner can achieve the ultimate in personal pleasure. So here we go!

1. The Paper Cut—As the name suggests, it's like licking a hair-line crack.

Not all pussies are exactly the same. Some display lots of flange on the outside and others keep it tucked away inside. In addition, it stands to reason that some are just larger than others and so on. If your partner has a really nice, tight pussy with no signs of the pastrami on show, then it's what we describe as being like a "paper cut", and this technique will help you to pleasure your partner's paper cut.

Your challenge here, before you get started, is to understand where her pussy is most sensitive. When all you have in front of you is the equivalent of a vertical pencil line and nothing else, then it's not easy without the experience that the Wise Cracks Team have provided here. First things first, you must be able to locate her clitoris before you get started. If it helps, you can just spread her pussy a little for orientational purposes. It's important that you hit the spot here, so be sure you know where it is. We recommend that you memorise it well and do not use any marker pens on her flesh as a reminder. Don't worry, because after a few attempts, eventually muscle memory will kick in, and finding it will become second nature and very natural. This is very similar to the experiences of learning to play a musical instrument; repetitive movement is recorded by your brain, and it eventually becomes an automatic response. The other thing you can do to help is to try to spot other natural signs close by her clitoris that might be there to help you. This could be marks on the skin like a small mole, maybe a particular odour or a love bite she received from a previous partner—just kidding!

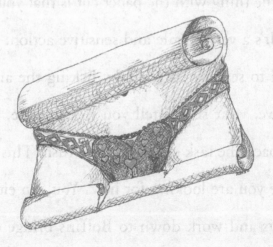

With this technique, your partner can be in almost any position she likes—on all fours with her arse in the air, laying down, or sitting on your face. It matters not. It takes more than just a parting of her legs to rearrange this pussy purely due to the way it is designed. It's guaranteed to stay tight throughout no matter what you do.

You will eventually recognise a theme across all of the techniques described here, and that is to take your time, be gentle, and don't go at it like a bull in a china shop. If your partner is sitting on you, then encourage her to thrust her pussy and also gyrate it slowly against your tongue.

Now the thing with the paper cut is that you need to be delicate. It's a very fragile and sensitive action. If you have ever tried to seal an envelope by licking the area smeared in adhesive, your senses tell you to be aware, and so you will approach the task subtly and not rush. This is the same technique you are looking for here. You can either start at her clitoris and work down to Boffins bridge or work up from Boffins bridge. Either way is okay, the reason being that your tongue puts no more pressure on her pussy than if you were breathing warm air onto it. Yes, that gentle. When licking, keep your tongue short and close to your lips. Use the closeness and warmth of your lips to increase the sensation.

You can practice, if you like, by placing a straw in your mouth and blowing gently through it onto your own skin. Try to find somewhere relatively sensitive to practice on, like the inside of your wrist or maybe your balls if you can reach. The technique requires no more energy than you'd use if you were wafting smoke onto her pussy. Believe it or not, the touch of your tongue should not deliver any more sensation than that. It's an ooze of pleasure, it's a soft summer breeze, it's a gentle and fragrant puff of curling passion. It simply has to be no more than a caress of love.

Once you're comfortable with the requirements of the technique, slowly hover your lips and tongue close to her pussy. As her intensity heightens at the thought of what is coming next, gently caress her pussy. Just keep it nice and static above her clit and tease it with the love smoke you are now wafting over it. Such intimacy is rare. She will begin to move a little on her arse and encourage you to be more forceful. Resist. Don't allow her to dominate. Eventually, as you move up and down her pussy, she will relax more, and the rapid muscle spasms will start to kick in. The inevitable will follow—she will orgasm. Her hips will thrust upwards as she pushes her cumming pussy into your face. At this point, you can, if you wish, abandon the gentle smoky caressing and roger her hard with your tongue until she can pleasure no more.

2. The Custard Bowl—This one's voluptuous and full of flavours.

The custard bowl is best carried out with your partner on her back and her pussy raised from the bed. With her legs wide open, you will need to be able to reach her pussy and, at the same time, gently open it by holding both of the sides. Pull her pussy open gently using both hands (fore and index fingers probably) to create a bowl effect. So, if your partner prefers to lie down, place a pillow under her hips to raise that pussy off the bed. If you prefer, you can lie down and your partner can position herself astride your face with her pussy very close to your mouth. In this position, she should pull open her pussy herself and hold it there to create a bowl effect. Yup, that's it! Try a little more stretch so you can see plenty of pink.

Get the picture?

Now, once the pussy is open and the shape is more or less correct, you start to work your tongue. Go for a long, pointed tongue, and make sure you touch only the sides of the bowl. No diving in there and licking deep into the love tunnel, okay? Keep it under control. Move the end point of your tongue slowly and gently. Try to move it in a clockwise direction from twelve o' clock slowly around to three and six o'clock, momentarily pausing on six. Don't lift your tongue from her pussy, okay? Keeping it slow and gentle, continue moving your tongue now towards nine and then gently on to twelve, back where you started.

When you reach the twelve o'clock position of her pussy, gently flick your tongue from side to side on the exposed clitoris. Listen carefully for any signs of whether you are hitting the right spot or not. Either way, don't stop, just keep going and focus on getting those juices flowing. Then carry on and repeat the above until your partner cums again and again and love custard is running all over your face; hence, the reference to custard bowl.

If your partner is sitting astride your face, you should be prepared to take over holding her pussy keeping in the shape of the bowl. It needs to keep its shape for this technique to work well. This requires some concentration, and she may not be able to continue when close to or when having an orgasm. Again, if she is sitting astride you, then you might also need to be prepared for her thrusting her pussy into your face as she gyrates with pleasure and groans uncontrollably.

Remember, it's you who is in control of the number, length, and intensity of her orgasms since you are driving the bus so to speak. Stay switched on at all times and try to feel those body movements and sounds she is putting out. When you hit a sensitive spot, then take notice and remember it. Be prepared to revisit the spot or spots over and over again.

Once there is no custard left, let her fall gently on her back as she takes your dick in her hand and directs it to her mouth, kissing it softly in appreciation. Smile. Now it's your turn.

3.   The crossroads—This one scored high with most of our volunteers.

If you follow this guide exactly, your partner is likely to be having the most intense and prolonged orgasms ever. Be prepared to score massive brownie points with this technique. In terms of positioning, you can position yourself however you wish as long as your tongue is at right angles to her pussy. That is key here. For best results, ask her to lie flat on her back with her legs supported and slightly apart. This position should provide maximum relaxation and allow her to float up as the depth of the orgasm penetrates her soul. It allows her to move freely unhindered without any concern. This is important and will only heighten the experience for both of you.

So, you now lie on your side and place your face close to her pussy. You must be able to reach and lick her clitoris, so you may need to elevate your head and possibly rest it on her thigh. Please make sure you are both comfortable before getting started.

She needs to be free to move her hands now, and your dick should be close to her mouth so that, when she starts to get excited (because you are doing a decent job), she may start to suck or rub your dick at the same time.

The thing is that, with this position, orgasms do tend to be strong and will cause her body to straighten initially before her back arches up while she screams intensely in pure delight. At this point, as you take her to the moon and back, I am afraid she isn't so interested in your dick but more in your tongue and what it is doing to her clit. So don't be disappointed if, in the execution process, it's all about her. You will get your chance later I assure you.

Okay, so once you're in position, make sure you have sight of her clit and that you can reach it without difficulty. With two fingers, expose the clit. Then reach over and moisten it slowly and affectionately by rubbing your tongue gently around it. When you are ready, just say hello by pushing your tongue against her clit. Hold it down for a second and then quickly release. You should be able to see the clit spring back into its natural place.

So now move to the side of her clit that is closest to you. Your tongue should now be at a crossroads position to her clit. Softly push the clit over with your tongue, bending it all the way down. Again, hold the pressure gently on it for a split second and then flick your tongue away to release it. Once again, her clit bounces back to its natural position. At this point you may wonder what the hell you are doing, but she will have started to feel something building inside her not quite like anything else. So now that you have mastered the push and flick technique, you just need to keep going at a speed you are both comfortable with. What you are looking for here is a lick, push, and flick technique. Remember the basic approach: lick, push, and flick; lick, push, and flick. Try to feel the rhythm of it until it rolls off the tongue so to speak.

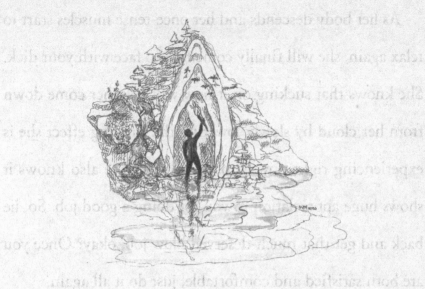

"I am sure that G spot is here somewhere!"

The build-up to orgasm is likely to be slow, but when it comes, it will come from deep within her. When you sense this, it's important that you don't change your rhythm, as consistency is important. It's that consistency that adds a bit of tantric control. The overall results of this technique are usually sensational. The orgasm spasm can last maybe one and a half to two minutes in real time, which really isn't bad going. Some of the volunteers also felt a distinct rise in body temperature as well as leg shaking. So be prepared to experience new things, maybe, with this technique.

As her body descends and her once-tense muscles start to relax again, she will finally come face to face with your dick. She knows that sucking on it now will help her come down from her cloud by slowly lowering the tingling effect she is experiencing right now across her body. She also knows it shows huge appreciation to you for doing a good job. So, lie back and get that much-deserved blow job, okay? Once you are both satisfied and comfortable, just do it all again.

4. **The Wheelbarrow—This requires the use of upper body strength, but it's amazing if you can pull it off.**

Let's hope you are feeling a bit athletic so you can enjoy this one to the max. This technique requires you both to be totally naked for the best results. Probably the best position to start this is for your partner to lie face down on a bed or table, whatever you are both most comfortable with. Get your partner to lift the top half of her body on her arms and place a cushion or cushions underneath her for support and comfort. What you need to be able to do is hold and raise both of your partner's legs ideally from above the knee and, as you lift, spread both legs nice and wide.

As you stand behind your partner with her legs now parted, you should now have a clear vision of her arse and pussy. How beautiful is that! Once you are comfortable and ready to start, reach forward with your tongue to ensure you are within touching distance of her pussy. Once this dry run is out of the way, you are able to take full control. Slowly, gently, and playfully give Boffins bridge a lick with your tongue before moving in to her pussy. We recommend you give it a good soaking to help get those juices flowing. This will let her know that the play is about to begin.

You may have to stretch a little based on the positioning of her legs, but slowly work your tongue towards the top of her pussy so you can reach her clit and give it a good soaking. Once you have reached this, again as you did with Boffins bridge, playfully flick your tongue gently around the clit. Try not to push too hard; it's not about penetration but about sensitivity and stimulation. Once the pleasure groaning starts, slowly reverse off her clit and back down the folds of her wet pussy all the way to Boffins bridge and rest. Repeat as desired.

Now the next bit is a game changer in oral terms and will probably raise your relationship intimacy even further. When you reach Boffins bridge, and with your tongue still gently caressing her, move further down to her nice pink arse. Again, resist penetration but gently flick your tongue around her arse, nice and easy as she becomes wetter and wetter and more excited. There is a chance that by now there may be some discomfort with her legs. Do the right thing and ask her. If this is the case, then get her to bend her legs and support herself on her knees but keep her legs still nicely apart.

This now gives you the opportunity to gently open her arse a little bit more so you can penetrate it deeper but still gently with your tongue. Again, take it nice and slow. Drag your tongue back across Boffins bridge, along her flaps, and towards her clit. The success of this is in the speed and the gentleness that you apply the technique. If it's too quick and maybe a bit rough, you won't get the best results. At all times, you have to be easy and gentle. Remember, lick long, lick everlasting. Do it right, and it will be something your partner will keep coming back for. In the end, she will prefer it to chocolate, with or without the nuts.

It won't be long before she starts to orgasm. The orgasm is likely to be long and protracted causing her legs to shake. Her body temperature will rise. She will jerk and writhe slightly, but if your technique is correct, it's you who is controlling her. Continue to gently move from her clit to her arse again and again until she can't take any more.

When her legs can't take anymore, and you need to change things, you have two options. You can take her gently from behind with your dick or you can allow her to show her appreciation by turning on you and sucking your now rock-hard dick. The Wise Cracks Team suggest that you do the right thing here and let her take the lead and do what she wants.

5. **The Cream Donut—It's simply everybody's favourite, and our instructions also cover vegetarian and vegan options.**

If any of you like to mix foodstuff with sex, then this one is for you. It does put the person doing the licking more in control and, as such, allows the licker to continue licking when his partner may ask you to stop as she is already exhausted and has more than enough beads of sweat running down and across her naked body.

For best results, your partner should lie nice and flat on her back if this is possible. Again, once the basic hygiene checks are done and you get the thumbs up that she is ready, you should stand or kneel so that you have full visibility of her pussy. You can move her legs so they are slightly apart. To be in position properly, you need to be able to see the full crack from Boffins bridge right up to her clitoris. If her outer lips are large, then it's worth trying to straighten them a bit and tidy the folds; otherwise, it could get messy. But please don't use any mechanical devices for this—like bulldog clips or staples! Keep it all gentle, easy, and sweet. What you are looking for is a nice tidy run from Boffins bridge to her clit.

Once you are both happy that the course is ready, reach for a aerosol can of dairy cream. We suggest, at this point, that if you suffer from diabetes, this may not be for you unless you can source a sugar-free version. It is not unusual that this technique can use up quite a lot of cream, and we don't want to aggravate your medical condition in any way. I will leave that to you to figure out, but please be careful.

Okay. With the cream in hand (and the top off), begin to slowly apply the cream onto the surface of the pussy. Aim for a nice straight line, following the route from Boffins bridge all the way to her clit. Once you actually start licking, you will follow the same route from the bottom to the top. Don't be too mean with the cream, okay? Take your time and apply it in a thick layer. The idea is that, when you are looking down on her pussy after the cream is applied, it looks like an artisan cream donut from a posh bake shop.

And what do we all do with a cream donut? Yes, we gently run our tongues along the top layer of the moist cream that lies teasingly and voluptuously in excess along the centre crack. We mischievously apply our tongues to it and playfully lick the excess cream off. I suggest that vegans find a suitable non-dairy alternative to the cream, perhaps a sauce or maybe some homemade chutney, but that might be a bit zingy, so please get your partner's permission first.

Okay, so whether it's cream or homemade chutney, we should now all be ready to go. Assume the position and, starting at Boffins bridge, move slowly along her pussy. Don't forget to look up occasionally so you can see the furrow you need to plough right there ahead of you. It won't be good for either of you if you start to wander off-piste through the trees so to speak. So, to ensure you stay on course, make sure you are familiar with the road ahead.

It is worth making you aware that you can apply this oral technique in two ways: a) by going in deep and scooping large batches of cream (or maybe the homemade chutney or brown sauce if you went for a vegan option) in one hit, or b) by slowly shaving layers of the cream or chutney with your tongue from her pussy just a bit at a time, teasing her as you go. Also be aware that with this technique the cream will start to melt due to her raising body heat. It will run into the gentle soft folds of her skin, getting mixed in with the folded pastrami. This is likely to provide some backend entertainment which, again, will only be good for you.

Either option is good, okay? It's just personal preference, and if you don't have one then try both. Why not?

Just a thought for those using homemade chutney or pickle—you may want to do a double hygiene check to make sure nothing else has inadvertently got mixed in there, if you know what I mean. Better have some wipes handy.

So now we are at the bit where we start to get on with the job in hand. Our cream is nicely laid out on her pussy, as pure as driven snow, or again the pickle, which will by now resemble more of a rocky road approach. But either way we can see where we are going. If you are ready now, place your tongue on Boffins bridge, slowly drag it along the crack, and remove as much cream or pickle as you are comfortable with. When you reach her clit, check that she is still comfortable. Depending on what option you went for, you may now need to apply more cream or, indeed, pickle.

Having fun? Then simply repeat the process until she has had multiple orgasms and is repeatedly begging you to stop. Just a thought—if you did take up the option to use chutney, you could always enhance it a little with some grated cheese, which puts a slightly different spin on the traditional British ploughman's lunch. Mmm ... yummy.

6.   **Trampolining—It is what it says on the tin but with a long enough tongue it can become more than that. Go on—give it a go!**

This technique is meant to be both playful and great fun. It is what it says on the tin and requires that you both have few or no inhibitions at all and are very comfortable with each other. As with all trampolining, there is more than one level. In the context of this technique, there are two levels. We'll describe both here.

Level One

More than one position can be used, but for beginners we advise the following technique. Your partner should be lying down on her back with her legs as high and as wide as is comfortable. Support can be provided for her back to help prop her up. As for the gymnasts out there, you can achieve the results of this technique if you are in a vertical "69" position, but your partner needs to be comfortable with hanging upside down placing her face almost on your dick as you perform the trampoline technique. If she is, then that's okay.

Before we actually start the trampolining, it's important that you are able to work your tongue almost in to the same style of an erect penis. It needs to be strong and hard and protruding from your mouth as much as possible. This technique is not designed for a flat or gentle tongue; in fact, the opposite. For a successful trampoline style, the tongue has to be rigid in order to successfully penetrate her pussy.

With your hard, protruding tongue now ready, place your head between her legs so you are aligned with her pussy. The movement you are looking for is a stabbing movement. If you're good to go, plunge your tongue in to her pussy and hold it there for maybe ten seconds. Slowly remove it completely. Again, hold for a second or two and plunge it in again. Again, wait a while before you remove it. Now slowly speed the process up. We are not looking for a frenzied approach here, but for a rhythm that is both relaxing for your partner and enjoyable for you both. Now you are trampolining!

Once you have trampolined six to eight times, you can start to push your tongue deeper—as deep as it will go into her pussy. Make sure your partner is still comfortable. If she is, begin to trampoline harder and deeper, again not in a frenzied way, but moving as quickly in and out as you are both comfortable with. Her sensitive inner pussy will become stimulated, and orgasm will begin to flow. Her body temperature will go up, and her pussy muscles will start to grip your tongue as you trampoline. This movement will lead to her having more and more prolonged orgasms.

Continue and repeat this process until you are both dripping in love juices and are exhausted.

Level Two

If you are in the mood and able to move to the next level, then simply drag your tongue across Boffins bridge, open her arse gently, and expose that beautiful pink flesh. Now slowly drive your rigid tongue in to that pink hollow and send her spinning off into Lala land. Now just keep going with the same technique, strokes, penetration depth, and speed as you used on her pussy. As the muscles in her arse slowly relax, you will be able to penetrate deeper and deeper with each thrust.

If you are extra good and she is enjoying it, you can move from her arse back to her pussy. Penetrate the pussy say five or six times and then move back to her arse and penetrate as before. If you followed the hygiene advice we provided earlier, there should be no concerns about cross contamination here. So, again, continue until she is totally satisfied and turns her attention on you. You can now simply lie back and let her pleasure you. You earned it.

7.   The Stamp—It's basic, but once you apply with care, you will both be stuck.

This technique requires the guy to use the full surface of his tongue. It is similar to licking a postage stamp or the way dog lovers are greeted by their pooches every day, with long, slow, warm, and wet strokes. We do not suggest for one moment that you take tips from your dog (or any other dog for that matter) or camp out at your local post office for stamp licking lessons. No. We suggest that you study the following easy-to-remember steps. You will learn all you need to know.

For this technique, you can manage in a number of positions. The most straightforward is for your partner to lie flat on her back and spread her legs so that you can access her pussy head on.

However, to make life a bit more interesting, the Wise Cracks Team suggest that you sit on the floor and lean against a wall. Your partner should stand with her pussy in front of you so it is within reach of your tongue. If, by any chance, you can do this so that she is in front of a floor mirror, then even better—for her anyway.

The mirror should be on wall behind you. She can support herself by placing her palms flat on the wall, and at the same time, she can watch herself throughout the experience. This will heighten the excitement, especially when she is close to having orgasm. Finally, when she cums, she will be able to vividly follow each and every one of her face muscles contorting in harmony with the muscles in her stomach and her pussy. It really is worth the small investment for a floor mirror if you don't have one.

As with all of our techniques, before you begin, please get comfortable. If you are sitting down on the floor, then use a cushion to sit on and maybe another behind your back if needed. This way you can simply relax and enjoy the experience more.

Once your partner has her knickers off and is close enough to your face, you may find it a good idea to reach out both arms and hold the tops of her legs or her buttocks. This does a couple of things. One, it will give you some extra support, and two, it will allow you to move her either away or closer to you as you lick her out.

Beware that, while you are carrying out this technique, she may have a tendency to writhe and thrust her pussy all over your face due to the high sensitivity she is experiencing. Clasping her thighs or buttocks gives you some control. Believe us—you need that control because, to deliver maximum effect that will result in joyous and explosive multiple orgasms, she needs to have her pussy against your face so you can position your tongue. Simple as that.

So similarly, to the way that a rodeo rider hangs on to his horse, at the penultimate moment, you will need to do the same. Once she builds up to climaxing, she'll gush all over your face. So, you see, spending a few quid on a floor mirror will be a good investment. Maybe, also when you are at the shop, you could pick up an extra towel or two as this technique may get a bit messy. During the trials, one couple participating got very wet indeed. The woman, who had never had a gusher before, experienced it for the first time during the stamp. It was totally unexpected. As a result, her partner for the trial, who had not stripped naked, had his shirt and trousers totally soaked in gushing cum, which as some of you may know, while not being totally unpleasant, does have a certain odour that can create a level of curiosity from others near you when you're on the bus going home. So, if we haven't mentioned it before, best to get naked and, of course, have a towel ready. Better still, shower afterwards if you can—of course together!

So now everything is in place, we can begin the process. With your tongue nice and flat, start to drag it along the lips of her pussy from Boffins bridge slowly and gently to her clit. As with all our techniques, take your time and be gentle. When doing so, apply pressure on your tongue by pulling her close to you. Once at the clit, you Need to hold it there for a second or two. You can release the pressure, which will allow her pussy to spring gently back. This is always a nice moment when you can look up and take a peep at those lovely tits just bouncing above your head. Try to also look over your shoulder into the mirror for a quick glance of her facial expression. Good, hey!

Now lift your tongue from her clit—so no touching—and go back down to Boffins bridge and repeat. Keeping your tongue nice and flat as you apply pressure to her pussy by motioning her forward closer to your face. If you have grabbed her by the arse, you can also build in a little trampolining here before you lick the full length of her pussy. Don't rush this, okay? And don't start behaving like a digging Donald. That's not how to do it. Simply try to ensure that you cover all of the pastrami that the pussy has on display. That said, don't be tempted to play around in any of the folds either; that is a different technique altogether. The success of the stamp technique is to maximize surface area. You need to cover the lot. Do it right, and you are bound to get soaking wet. Other than the technique itself, the other bit of advice that the Wise Cracks Team can give you is to be prepared for anything. And we mean anything. Administered properly, this technique can deliver quite extraordinary results. She won't even recognise herself afterwards. She could maybe even be a little bit embarrassed by the amount of noise she generates let alone the high volumes of love juice she has just covered you in. No hair gel can compete, I assure you.

So be nice. Make sure she is relaxed and not feeling awkward.

Then it's your turn. However you decide to continue having fun is up to you, but whatever you choose, it will all be unforgettable and hopefully the start of a proper stamp collection.

8. The Bishop's Finger—This one's mainly aimed at those more experienced in cunnilingus as it requires a bit of space.

First and foremost, as a safety precaution, please remove any rings and maybe wrist watches and put them to one side. And ensure your fingernails are nicely clipped. The bishop's finger technique is best suited to those who want a rapid orgasm. Its fast, furious, and can get very wet and slippery. Also, if the woman is a squirter, then this position is ideal for maximising this phenomenon. If you follow the steps carefully, your partner will explode into orgasm heaven with a bang. Again, comfort and cleanliness are paramount. For your safety, you may wish to wear goggles to protect you from the hysterical wave of orgasmic delight that is about to wash over you.

Since there tends to be a lot of instantaneous and uncontrolled leg movement with this method, it is suggested that your partner lie nice and flat with a pillow under her hips. If her pussy is nicely elevated, you will easily be able to reach its full length. So, everything is visible from her clit all the way down through the folds of pastrami to Boffins bridge. Just in case squirting should occur, you should also make sure that you are safely distanced away from any live electrical appliances. As you know, electrics and "jing juice" don't mix, and we don't want anybody being rushed to A&E unnecessarily. The other thing you simply must to do is wash your hands thoroughly. Nobody wants the chance of infection. For a woman, this area is very sensitive, and cleanliness is an absolute must.

So now that your partner is nice and comfortable, you should position yourself with your head between her legs facing directly at her pussy. Move your head slightly off centre as you will need a little bit of space for the bishop's finger once you get going. Once you are in position, slowly moisten all of her pussy with your tongue. Use nice, long, gentle strokes, easing your way from Boffins bridge up to her clit—nice and slow, up and down, trying not to take your tongue off her pussy. Hopefully the pastrami isn't too salty for your liking. If it is, give it a little wipe.

Now this is a good time to introduce the bishop's finger. You will need to wet the finger or fingers of your choice depending on her preferred comfort levels. Let's assume it's a single finger for this exercise. As you moisten the finger with your tongue, let her watch as you run your tongue over it. It's even better if you can wet your finger using her tongue! On seeing this, her reaction should be to open her eyes wider than normal as the intensity heightens. You must not let the moment go cold by taking your eye off the main event, so keep the finger licking to no more than a couple of seconds.

Remember, as a precaution, you may want to remove the bishop's ring and possibly any other precious heirlooms.

Moving slowly and gently, break the seal of her pussy with your finger and slowly move it inside her. At the same time, you need to be lowering your face to her pussy and beginning to lick her. Start the licking as before, slowly and easily, but this time from about halfway up her pussy to her clit. Keep your tongue nice and flat. From Boffins bridge to where you started licking her is now reserved for the bishop's finger. You are going for maximum surface area coverage with your tongue as you did with the stamp. At the same time, you should now be gently moving your finger in and out of the bottom part of her pussy.

We suggest you start this in a controlled manner until you know she is comfortable and is taking the rogering that your finger is giving her well within her stride. If that is the case, you can always slip in a naughty second finger. With this technique, orgasm is achieved through playing with her both internally and externally, moving simultaneously. If she is comfortable, then speed up the process. It may get to a frenzy depending on what she allows. Remember at all times that it's about satisfying her. Like it or not, it's all about her, and your fun will have to wait. But believe us, it will be worth waiting for.

9. The Chocolate Nut Sunday—This one's for when you get home from church obviously.

For most who live in the Western world, one of the better days in any week is Sunday. I know it's not for everyone, and this could be because of religion, having to work on Sundays, or whatever, but most of us generally see Sunday as a relaxing day. Also, we do of course understand that your relaxing day might be a different day, but as long as we all have one, that's fine. So, if it's okay with you, we will stay with Sunday as the relaxing day for this technique.

So, let's imagine it's a nice warm Sunday morning, and you have just returned from a bit of a run in the local park. You get home and are expecting a nice shower and possibly some brunch before settling down into the rest of the day. Your clothes are off and you're making your way to the shower. While the water is running, getting up to your preferred temperature, you glance momentarily and admire your hard work and dedication to fitness in the mirror. Once you have had a good shower, you dry off, taking your time since you don't want to disturb your partner, who is still in bed. Once dry, and with the towel around your waist, you make your way to the bedroom where your partner is lying on the bed. There's nothing unusual in any of that so far except that you notice she has a tub of spreadable chocolate sauce at her side. So what are your first impressions? "That looks interesting!" or "What has she been doing with that?" Or, indeed, "What is she going to do with that?" It takes a little time, but the confusion steadily creeps towards trust, and it doesn't take long before you surrender totally.

Eventually, as you approach her, she asks you if you would like a massage after your workout. You respond, "Absolutely, since you are asking." She gestures to you come onto the bed, and she asks you lie chest down, which you do without any argument at all. She asks you to open your legs, and again, you give her no argument at all. Then something happens that you were not necessarily expecting. She asks you to bring your knees up in order to raise your butt in the air slightly. At this point, you have a mixed cocktail of emotions running through your body, all of which are contributing to the sizeable erection you are experiencing. But do you trust her? Does it matter?

Okay, now she finally has you in position. You have effectively offered yourself to her totally and have given her permission to do whatever she wishes to do with you. Now you will recall you saw her semi hiding the spreadable chocolate sauce. The good news is that, within a few seconds, it will be totally clear what she is going to do with it. With your nuts now hanging freely and not being hindered by your erect dick, which is out of the way, she begins to caress and massage your nuts—just a little. The massage intensifies as she grabs a handful of the chocolate sauce and begins to smear it on your nuts. Gently she covers your nuts in the sauce as they limply and defencelessly hang there. It's a helpless situation for you as you can't really get out of it. You have to play along. Within a couple of minutes, your nuts are totally covered in the sauce. Additionally, she's even dabbed some around your arse.

She puts the container of chocolate sauce down softly by your side. Now you know step one is complete. At this point, you will be fantasising about what she is going to do with your rock-hard dick. Fully understandable. Her hand slides in from your side, and she takes your dick in her palm and gently closes it. Moving it gently, she caresses it up and down for a brief moment. Then, with a playful slap on your arse, she demands that you turn over onto your back. As you oblige, your balls flop between your legs, and your dick remains standing proud. With full unfettered access, she will now bend forward and begin to lick the chocolate sauce from your balls. Her tongue will gently remove all traces while, at the same time, she tosses your manhood. As you begin to orgasm, she will move her mouth to place her lips above the tip of your dick and await the arrival of your man jam, allowing it to splash all over her pouting pink lips and soft facial skin. The perfect chocolate Sunday—chocolate sauce and a splash of added man jam.

10. The "69"—A default position, possibly, when it comes to oral sex, and much underrated by many, but not in our book!

Well, did we save the best for last? Arguably we may have; it's debatable. It is indeed a wonderful experience and gives you both the ultimate orgasmic pleasure of being able to both come at the same time. That is a truly beautiful moment in any relationship. Pleasure being given in equal measure by two people so that that their bodies are working in a naturally organic, coordinated rhythm that is timed to deliver an explosion of love juices simultaneously. There can't be anything better. And the view is really quite exceptional for both of you. She is now looking down your shaft at your balls, which are flicking all over the place as she takes your dick down her throat. While this is happening, you get to stare at both sides of Boffins bridge as you skilfully work your tongue from her arse up to her clit. We all agree that the Northern Lights are also thought of as an unbeatable spectacle, but even they don't get close to this view when both of you are in full uncontrollable motion. That said, this position isn't everybody's cup of tea. Strange but true. Or it could be that you are just not doing it right, in which case you should read on.

Firstly, though, this technique needs that little bit of extra attention when it comes to comfort and cleanliness. The technique itself is straight forward enough, so when you analyse why some people don't like it, it's most likely down to comfort and cleanliness. This oral option is by far the most common of all. It's a default for when your partner says, "Let's have some oral sex." Everyone assumes automatically it's a reference to having a "69". So, as a consequence, due to the spontaneous reaction, there tends to be less care taken to cleanliness by both partners, and that can lead to a bit of disappointment. So, if you want to try this, make sure both of you treat it with respect. Enjoy some extended foreplay. You could consider washing each other's genitals and even trimming a bit of each other's bush, maybe, to help with the visual effects. Whatever you do, though, being clean and being neat is paramount and is an important part of the art of a good "69". It's a blend of both technique and grooming. Rushing it just doesn't do it justice. So, let's walk through it.

Are you comfortable? Usually this starts with both of you being naked or possibly wearing suitable clothes that give both of you the access you need to perform. There are a number of positions. You can lie side by side or one on top of the other. Or one of you can be standing vertically and the other can hang from the other's shoulders. Whatever your preference, you must be head to toe, essentially with your mouths in close proximity to the other's genitals.

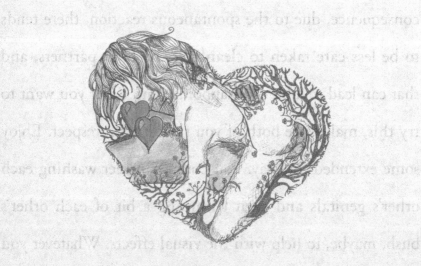

Let's assume you have bathed or showered together and trimmed each other's bush as we suggested earlier, remembering to tidy those loose hairs. Couples can get carried away during the "69" process and have been known to swallow the odd fur ball accidentally, which can be uncomfortable and off-putting. If the victim who is receiving the fur ball is of weak constitution, it can stop the process totally, which is unfortunate. It may even require the need for a respiratory technique like the "hind-lick" manoeuvre to help in removing the fur ball if choking starts to occur. Please note that the hind-lick manoeuvre is not a technique provided by the Wise Cracks Team; while it can be effective, it has nothing to do with us.

So, we are all happy and ready to go. As there is role play for you and your partner, we have separated the steps each of you will follow so we won't confuse anybody.

Guys

As with so many of our techniques, we recommend that you play initially with the clit and then move quickly and gently down to her arse and flick your tongue softly around the rim. Once you start to get a reaction, gently move your tongue from her arse, easing your way through the lips to pastrami land up to the top of her pussy. Again, flick or gyrate your tongue on or around her clit.

Ladies

While this is going, on you should now have commenced running your tongue in a circular movement around the top of his dick. Rather than taking the full length in to your mouth in one hit, you should take your time and inch your way down the shaft, teasing and moisturising as you go. So, circumvent the rim at the top of the dick and swallow about fifteen millimeters at a time until it is all in. It's not for everyone, but you could give a playful bite at this point just to wake him up.

Both of You

If you take your time with these techniques, you will soon be close to orgasm. At that point, we recommend you go up a couple of gears to heighten the pleasure. Very soon what happens next will be out of your control. Juices will be cascading down and around your faces, and both of your mouths will fill with sweet-scented love juice. You will gasp for air and fall back into one of the most relaxing frames of mind ever achieved. As a practical tip, you may want to be prepared with some spare sheets or towels as there is bound to be a lot of juice around, possibly even a bit of squirting, so sheets may even need to be changed.

A SCORE SHEET

Yes, we even have a score sheet for each of the ten recommended techniques. Use the scoresheets to rank the techniques after you have tried them. You can keep notes about your own and your partner's experiences and levels of enjoyment. In addition, you can record any feedback or general notes or observations that may be useful in future. Ultimately, keeping a record will hopefully help you improve upon your experiences for the next time and the time after that.

Technique	Your Performance Rating	Your Partners Performance Rating	Favourite Moment	Overall Enjoyment
The Paper Cut				
The Custard Bowl				
The Cross Roads				
The Wheel Barrow				
The Cream Donut				
Trampolining				
The Stamp				
The Bishops Finger				
The Chocolate Nut Sunday				
The 69				

THE LAST WORD

Well, that was a bit of a marathon, wasn't it? A lot of fun though. If you have managed to try and perfect all ten techniques, then you must have a grin on your face as wide as the Grand Canyon. You will have your favourites as well, of course, but hopefully on any day at any time, you will find a slot for any one of the ten, as they all have their place.

The key to a happy sex life is, of course, down to your emotional connection with your partner. Our guide helps you to share the love and respect you have for each other and then spice it up. And we do that with variety in our approach and techniques. If you are not careful, sex can become boring if you follow the same old routine. So, the key here is to keep trying the different techniques in different ways and situations. Also, keep having fun. Life is too short and at times far too serious for anything else. Find time for each other, hold hands, be affectionate, and show each other you care.

The other bit of good news is that the Wise Cracks Team will be working to provide you with other useful and informative techniques that will continue to make you both giggle and, at the same time, help you along with your sex lives. So watch out for further releases.

You probably get the idea that we are a bit more edgy than the rest when it comes to passing on these useful tips. And that won't change. We are committed to being informative but also to combining our information with fun. It's our way of putting smiles on the faces of the people we share this planet with. Being able to perform good oral sex is the best vaccine for any relationship, be it new or old, even when it's a bit bruised or tender for whatever reason. So, our mission is to help by showing ways for you to enhance, improve, and possibly fix things. We will continue to do that in our unique way for as long as you continue to read our stuff.

From the Wise Cracks Team, thank you for your time. We hope you enjoyed reading this as much as we enjoyed producing it.

"Mmmm ... stick!y"

WISE CRACKS Ltd.

CPSIA information can be obtained
at www.ICGtesting.com
Printed in the USA
LVHW100845041221
705161LV00007B/9

9 781984 594525